Aircraft 1950s

Memory Lane

The Lockheed U2 was a high-altitude spy plane used by the USAF and CIA between 1955 and 1989.

Compiled by Hugh Morrison

Montpelier Publishing

Cover pictures

Front cover (clockwise from left): Apache Longbow. Hawker Hurricane. Boeing 747. Piper Cub. F16. Douglas DC4.

Rear cover (clockwise from top): Boeing 707. Chinook. Bell 47G. F4 Phantom. F84 Thunderstreak. Piper PA23.

Image credits: Patrick Nugent, US Army, Kitmasterbloke, Ken Fielding, Tim Felce, Tomas del Coro, Ken Mist, A. Hunt, Peter Bakema, Matthew Field, National Aviation Museum of the USA, Aero Icarus, Julian Herzog, Bene Riobo, Richard Snyder, Roslyn Ward, Alan Wilson, Altair78, Geoff McKay, Mike Freer, Dale Coleman, Pedro Aragao, John5199, Aeroprints, Alf van Beem, Eduard Marmet, National Navy Aviation Museum, Pedro Aragao, P.J. Sime, Pseudopanax, Bob Adams, J.G. Nelson, Adrian Pingstone, US Marine Corps, Matthew Seafeldt, A.K. Benson, Andy Dunaway, J.M. Eddins Jr, Chris Lofting, Doug Green, Mike Buytas, Phil Major, Torsten Maiwald, W.M. Welch, Q. Stone, Peng Chen, D. Miller, Alan Lebeda, US Navy, Andrew Thomas, Montague Smith, Mike Jones, Milborne One, Ralf Manteufel, Dennis James.

ISBN: 9798308098935

Published in Great Britain by Montpelier Publishing.

Printed and distributed by Amazon.

This edition © 2025. All rights reserved.

The 1940s

Technical cutaway of a Spitfire. The Spitfire was Britain's premier fighter aircraft in service with the RAF from 1936 to 1957.

The Bell P59 Airacomet was the first US jet fighter, introduced in 1942.

The Gloster Meteor, the RAF's first jet fighter, introduced in 1943. It was the only Allied jet fighter to engage in combat in the Second World War.

Left: the Hawker Hurricane was the RAF's rival to the Spitfire. Introduced in 1937, it rose to fame in the Battle of Britain in 1940. It featured a Merlin II engine, two Vickers and one Browning machine gun.

The P-47 Thunderbolt was the main US fighter from 1941 to 1945. It was armed with six M2 Browning machine guns and had a top speed of 412 mph.

The USAF P-51 Mustang was in service during World War Two and the Korean War. It last flew operationally in 1984 with the Dominican Air Force.

The Avro Lancaster was the main British bomber of WW2. It had four Merlin engines and could carry up to 12,000 lb of 'blockbuster' bombs.

The DeHavilland Mosquito was a highly adaptable twin engined RAF fighter- bomber made largely from plywood.

The B-29 Superfortress was the main US bomber of WW2. It is the only bomber to have used nuclear weapons in combat, in the bombing of Hiroshima and Nagasaki.

The Douglas C47 Skytrain, also known as the Dakota was a military transport plane also used by civilian airlines. Here it is shown with USAF 'invasion stripes' to prevent friendly fire during the D-Day landings.

The Handley Page Halifax complemented the Lancaster as one of the RAF's main heavy bombers. Introduced in 1940, it served throughout WW2 and was adapted for post-war cargo duties including the Berlin Airlift of 1948.

The US Navy's M-Class blimps (non-rigid airship) were launched in 1944 for anti-submarine duties in US coastal waters. They had a top speed of 80mph and were armed with an M2 machine gun and depth charges.

The Lockheed Constellation ('Connie') was one of the main US civilian airliners of the 1940s. They were used during the Berlin Airlift of 1948.

Right: the Piper Cub was known as the 'Ford Model T of the Air' due to its popularity in the USA. It was produced from 1938 to 1947 and had a flat-four piston engine.

The Cesna 140 had an 85hp engine, metal body and fabric wings. It was produced between 1946 and 1951.

The Douglas DC4 was one of the most popular post-war prop airliners. It had four Pratt and Whitney 1450hp engines and a maximum speed of 280mph.

The Handley-Page Hermes was a British prop airliner built 1945-51 for BOAC. It had four Bristol Hercules radial engines, later changed to Bristol Theseus turboprops.

The Bristol Freighter, with front loading nose, was developed for war service but did not go into use until 1946. It proved popular as a short-haul car transporter especially across the English Channel.

The Sikorsky R4 was the first mass-produced helicopter, introduced in 1942. In Britain it was known as the Hoverfly.

The Boeing Stearman was first flown by US forces in the 1930s but was obsolete by 1945. It became a popular civilian aircraft in the post-war era particularly for use as a 'crop duster' by farmers.

The DeHavilland Vampire was Britain's second jet fighter, and went into service in 1946. It was the first RAF jet to exceed 500mph and set a world altitude record of 59,446 feet in 1948.

The 1950s

The Hawker Hunter entered service with the RAF in 1950. It was the first British swept-wing fighter and set the world speed record at 727.63 mph in 1953.

The Gloster Javelin was the RAF's first all-weather interceptor, introduced in 1956. It featured delta wings, radar and ejector seats and later models were armed with air-to-air missiles.

The F-86 Sabre was the first US swept-wing fighter and first saw service in the Korean War. It was armed with six M3 Browning machine guns and two unguided rockets.

The USAF's F84 Thunderstreak entered service in 1954 and was powered by the Wright J65 turboengine. In 1955 it set a record flying from Los Angeles to New York in 3 hours 44 minutes.

The Avro-Canada Canuck was the only Canadian jet fighter to be mass produced. Launched in 1950 it had two Rolls Royce Avon engines. In 1952 it became the first straight-wing fighter to break the sound barrier.

The Lockheed F94 Starfire entered service with the USAF in 1950. It had an afterburner to increase thrust, and a Fire Control System for automated gunnery.

The English Electric Canberra was the RAF's successor to the Mosquito fighter-bomber. In 1951 it became the first jet plane to make a non-stop transatlantic flight. It was also used by the USAF as the B-57 Canberra.

The RAF's Supermarine Swift was plagued by technical problems probably due to its rushed development during the Korean War. It did however set the world speed record at 737 mph in 1953.

The US Navy's Douglas A-4 Skyhawk had a long production run (1954-79) and saw service in the Vietnam War. It was one of the first air-to-air refueling planes. Armed with nuclear weapons, it had the same payload capacity as the B-17 bomber from WW2.

The Douglas Skyray, introduced in 1956, was the first US Navy fighter to break the sound barrier. It featured delta wings and a top speed of 752 mph.

The McDonnell F2H Banshee was used by the US Navy and Marines as well as the Royal Canadian Navy. One of the main fighters of the Korean War, it featured bulletproof glass, air-conditioning, and folding wings for storage on aircraft carriers.

The McDonnell F3H Demon went into service with the US Navy in 1956. Although it had innovations such as an adustable nose cone it suffered from technical problems and was nicknamed the 'lead sled' due to its low power to weight ratio.

Britain's De Havilland Comet was the world's first jet airliner. It went into service in 1952 and was eventually retired in 1979. It was known for its smooth ride and had an innovative pressurised fuel system enabling fast refills.

The Vickers Viscount was introduced in 1953 and was the first turboprop airliner. It was built to carry 32 passengers at a top speed of 200mph. It had unusually large oval windows and was known for its low noise levels.

The Bristol Britannia turboprop, introduced in 1957, was known as the 'Whispering Giant' due its low noise levels. Although used on the London-Sydney route it was soon superceded by faster jet airliners.

The USA's Boeing 707 was one of the longest serving jet liners, in civilian use from 1958 to 2019. It was the first plane to have six-abreast seating, leading to lower air fares and the start of the 'jet age'.

Produced from 1958 to 1972, the Douglas DC8 proved very popular and at time of writing (2025) is still in use as a freighter. In 1961 it became the first civilian airliner to break the sound barrier in a controlled dive.

The Boeing B-52 Stratofortress nuclear bomber has been in continuous service with the USAF since 1955. One of the largest and heaviest planes in the world, it has been described as the biggest step forward in US military technology since the adoption of the rifle.

The Bell 47 helicopter was introduced in 1946 and was popular throughout the 1950s. In the US Army it was called the H-13 Sioux. In 1950 it became the first helicopter to fly over the Alps and in 1958 it became the first TV news helicopter.

The Piper PA23 Apache was introduced in 1952 and was a popular four seater, twin engine plane for private and light commercial use until the 1980s.

The Beechcraft Twin Bonanza, also known as the L23 Seminole, was introduced in 1951. It was the first light aircraft to have seatbelts and gained a reputation as a solid, safe aeroplane.

The 1960s

The McDonnell Douglas F-4 Phantom was the most widely produced US fighter of the Cold War era between 1961 and 1996. It was used extensively during the Vietnam War.

The F-111 Aardvark, introduced in 1967, featured variable-sweep wings, turbofan afterburners and terrain-following radar to allow high speed flight at low altitude. It saw service in Vietnam with the USAF and the Royal Australian Air Force.

The Northrop F-5 Freedom Fighter was produced between 1959 and 1987 and was primarily used by the US Navy and NATO forces. It was designed as a small, economical fighter and trainer.

Britain's Hawker Harrier jump-jet was the world's first VSTOL (Vertical/Short Takeoff and Landing) plane. It entered service with the RAF in 1969 and was used in the Falklands War.

The English Electric Lightning unusually featured two Rolls Royce Avon turbojet engines staggered within the fuselage. It was able to climb almost vertically and was the first British fighter to reach Mach 2.

The RAF's Blackburn Buccaneer was launched in 1962. Fitted with anti-ship missiles, it was intended to combat small Russian cruisers, and later saw action in the First Gulf War.

The A-7 Corsair was a small, economic fighter capable of subsonic speed only. It went into service in 1967 and saw service in Vietnam and the First Gulf War.

The A-5 Vigilante could fly at up to Mach 2 and was the first bomber to have a digital computer. It was introduced in 1961 and saw service in Vietnam; many were used for reconnaissance.

The Folland Gnat was designed as a light fighter plane for the RAF, introduced in 1962. It was mainly used as a trainer, but saw active service with the Indian Air Force in the Indo-Pakistan War of 1965.

The Sea Vixen FAW2 entered service with the Royal Navy in 1964. It had an unusual off-centre cockpit and was fitted with four 'red top' heat seeking missiles. Some were also converted to unmanned drones.

The Hawker Siddeley Trident was introduced in 1964 for BEA (British European Airways). It featured a t-tail and was the first tri-jet, with three rear-mounted Rolls Royce Spey engines.

The Vickers VC10, introduced in 1962, saw service with the RAF as well as civil airlines. It performed well in 'hot and high' conditions making it popular with routes to tropical and mountainous destinations.

The British Aircraft Corporation (BAC) 1-11 went into service in 1965. A 160 seater intended for short-haul routes, the majority were bought by American Airlines.

The Handley Page Jetstream was a small 12 seater British twin turboprop liner introduced in 1968, which proved very popular on American short-haul and commuter routes.

The Short Belfast was a heavy-lift freighter introduced in 1964. Only ten were made, but they proved popular as transporter planes for the RAF as well as civilian use. It was the first large plane to be designed with automatic landing equipment.

The Britten-Norman BN2 Islander was introduced in 1967 and became a popular short-hop transporter still in use today.

The Boeing 727 tri-jet was introduced in 1964 and was designed for use in smaller airports. It featured nosewheel brakes which reduced stopping distances for short runways.

The McDonnell Douglas DC9 entered service in 1965 and was designed for short-haul routes. It could accommodate up to 135 passengers. It was the first jet to be fitted with a Head Up Display where instrument readings are projected on to the pilot's windscreen.

The Grumman Gulfstream II set the standard for the modern private jet when it was introduced in 1966. it was also used as a training plane for NASA's Space Shuttle pilots.

Probably the most iconic helicopter ever produced, the Boeing CH-47 Chinook was launched in 1962 and saw extensive service in the Vietnam War; it remains in service with the US and British military in 2025.

The Sikorsky SH-3 Sea King helicopter was introduced in 1961. It set the world helicopter speed record at 210 mph in 1962. It was widely adopted for both military and civil use, particularly air-sea rescue.

The 1970s

The Hawker-Siddeley T1 Hawk entered service as a trainer with the RAF in 1976. It is best known as the plane used by the RAF's Red Arrows display team. In the USA it was known as the T-45 Goshawk.

The Tornado, built for the British, Italian and German airforces went into service in 1979. It was a versatile fighter-bomber with variable wing-swing, and saw action in the two Gulf Wars.

The Jaguar was a joint French/British design which was launched in 1973. It was praised for its reliabillity and required only very narrow strips for take-off and landing, enabling it to use roads instead of airfields in an emergency.

The British Westland Lynx helicopter went into service in 1977 and holds the world helicopter speed record of 249mph. It is fully acrobatic and able to perform loops and rolls.

The Hawker-Siddeley Nimrod NR2 was an RAF signals/intelligence gathering plane which went into service in 1975. Its existence was not officially acknowledged until after the Cold War had ended.

The F-15 Eagle has been in service with the USAF since 1976 and is one of the most popular and versatile jet fighters ever built. It features radar-guided missiles and additional fuel tanks for longer missions.

The Lockheed S-3 Viking was a small carrier-based plane with high fuel efficiency. Introduced in 1974, it saw service in the First Gulf War and the Yugoslavian conflicts of the 1990s.

The Boeing E3 Sentry was introduced to the USAF in 1977. It has a distinctive rotating radar dome and is used for command/control operations. It is also known as AWACS (Airborne Warning and Control System).

The F-16 Fighting Falcon (also known as the Viper) was launched in 1979, it is the world's most popular fixed-wing jet fighter, with over 2000 still in use. It is used by the USAF Thunderbirds display team.

The F-14 Tomcat, built by Grumman in the USA, went into service in 1974. It featured an infra-red navigation system for night fighting, and laser-guided missiles. It was featured in the 1986 movie *Top Gun*.

The McDonnell-Douglas DC-10 was a widely used tri-jet which entered service in 1971. It suffered from early technical problems and following a major crash in 1979 the planes were taken out of service. Following a major overhaul, the planes stayed in use until 2014.

The Lockheed L-1011 Tristar was a wide-body (two aisles) tri-jet which went into service in 1972. It could seat 400 and had a lower and upper deck. As of 2025 only one is left in use, used for launching space rockets at high altitude.

The Boeing 747, introduced in 1970, was the first 'jumbo jet', with a double aisle and two decks, carrying up to 400 passengers on long haul routes. The plane dominated the industry for many years and was in production until 2023.

The Cessna 152 was introduced in 1977 and soon became popular. Fueled by avgas, it was built largely from aluminium and powered by a 110hp Lycoming engine. Many were used as dual-control training planes for new pilots.

The joint British-French produced supersonic airliner Concorde went into service in 1976. Known for its distinctive tilting nose-cone, it could travel between London and New York City in under three hours. It went out of service in 2003.

The Grumman American AA-5 was a four seater light aircraft introduced in 1971. it had a 150 hp Lycoming engine with a 160 mph top speed. It featured bonded aluminium wings and a honeycomb fuselage combining lightness and strength.

The Beechcraft Duchess introduced in 1977, was an economical twin engine trainer with all-metal honeycomb fuselage and twin Lycoming engines. The t-tail design provided additional stability. It remains in use as a popular trainer with flying schools.

The Scottish Aviation Bulldog was launched in 1972 and saw service as a two-seater side-by-side trainer with the RAF University Air Squadrons and the Swedish air force. Although designed to be able to carry machine guns and a small missile/bomb load, it was never used in combat and went out of service in 2001.

The Bell Jetranger was introduced in 1971 and proved popular with police forces and TV news companies in the USA. In 1982 a Jetranger became the first helicopter to fly around the world, taking 29 days.

The Britten-Norman Trislander entered service in 1971. Designed as an economical short-hop passenger plane, it was particularly popular on routes between Britain's Channel Islands as well as in the islands of the West Indies.

The Chotia Weedhopper was one of several brands of 'ultralight' aircraft introduced in the 1970s. Designed for home construction, it was powered by a 28hp Rotax engine giving a top speed of 55 mph, and it required only 100' for takeoff and landing.

The 1980s

The Harrier II entered service with the RAF in 1987. An updated version of the Harrier jump-jet, it featured an enemy radar-blocking system and all main controls on a single stick. It was armed with AIM-19 Sidewinder missiles. It served in the two Gulf Wars, the Iraq War and the Afghanistan War.

The FA/-18 Hornet is a multirole fighter/attack jet introduced in 1983 and still in service with the USAF. It has a top speed of Mach 1.8 and is armed with Sidewinder, Sparrow and Skyflash missiles.

The USAF's B-2 'Stealth' heavy bomber first flew in 1989. It features anti-radar-detection systems and can carry up to 40,000lb of bombs including the MOP 'bunker buster' 30,000lb bomb. It was first used in combat during the Kosovo War.

The Bell-Boeing V22 Osprey was first flown in 1988 and was intended to bridge the gap between helicopters and fighter jets. It uses tilt-rotors which can be adjusted for forward flight, hovering or vertical take-off/landing.

The Short Tucano is a basic two seater turboprop trainer introduced to the RAF in 1988. A combat-ready version with missile capability was produced for the Kuwait Air Force.

The F117 Nighthawk was introduced in 1983 and was designed to evade radar systems and to intercept surface-to-air missiles.It first engaged in combat in the 1989 US invasion of Panama.

The Boeing 757 narrow-body dual-engine jet liner entered service with Eastern Airlines in 1983. it has proved highly popular and is also in use as a cargo plane and as the US military's C32 transporter.

The Boeing 767 first went into service with United Airlines in 1982. Able to seat 216 passengers with a 4500 mile range it has proved ideal for long-haul routes.

The McDonnell-Douglas MD80 was launched in 1980 by Swissair on the Zurich-London route. It seats 173 people and is powered by two Pratt and Whitney Turbofan engines giving high fuel economy.

The Cessna Caravan was launched in 1986 and seats 9 in an unpressurised cabin. It is used for flight training, cargo and skydiving. It is powered by a single Pratt and Whitney turboprop.

The Beechcraft Starship, launched in 1989, had rear tractor (push) propellors, carbon fibre body and canard dual wing configuration. Seating 8, it was used for business travel but went out of production in 1995.

The Mooney M20K was one of a long line of Mooney planes dating back to the 1940s. Launched in 1986, it had a top speed of 252mph and a 210hp Porsche engine. Able to seat three passengers, it was a popular private-transportation plane.

The Boeing Apache helicopter began service with the US Army in 1986 and has been used by many other forces including Britain's Army Air Corps. It is equipped with anti-tank and air-to-air missiles and first saw action in the US invasion of Panama.

The McDonnell Douglas 520N helicopter was launched in 1989. It had no tail rotor, but instead used a hidden fan which resulted in much less engine noise.

The Westland 30 went into service with British Airways in 1982, supporting oil rigs in the North Sea as well as the passenger route to the Scilly Isles. It was also used to transport passengers between downtown New York City and JFK airport.

Other Memory Lane titles...
Available online at Amazon and other good booksellers

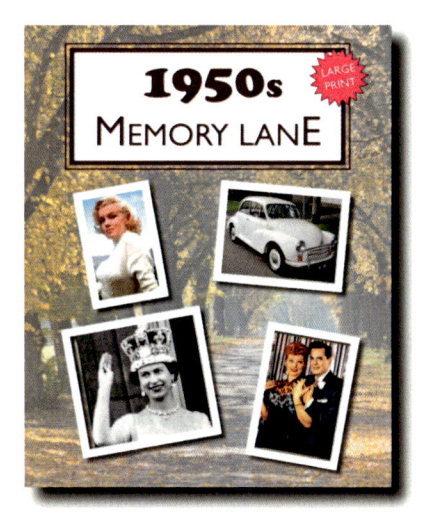

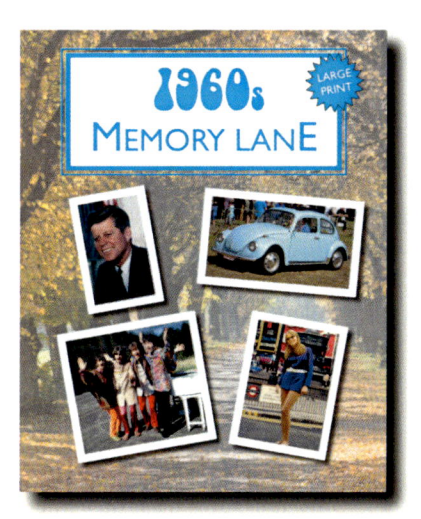

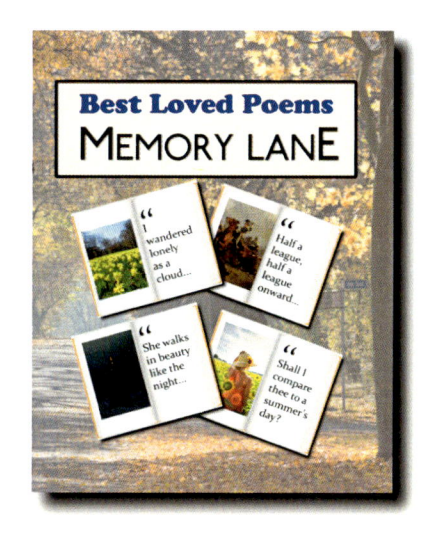

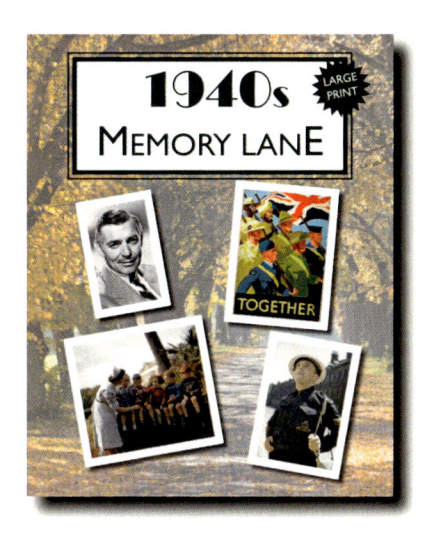

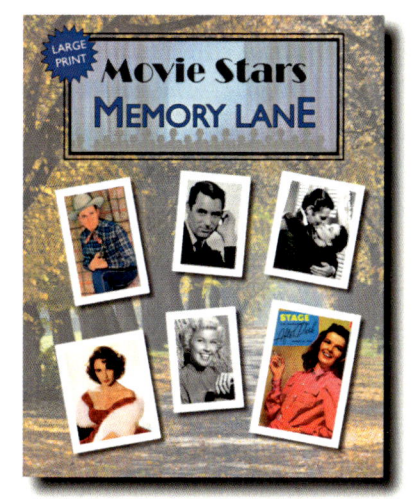

Manufactured by Amazon.ca
Acheson, AB

15688881R00026